NATIONAL GEOGRAPHIC

A Good Place to Live

Marvin Buckley

My town is a good place to live.

People keep my town clean.

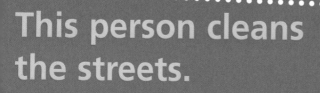

street cleaner

This person cleans
the streets.

trash collector

This person takes away the trash.

yard worker

This person cuts the grass in the park.

People keep my town safe.

police officer

This person directs traffic.

fire fighter

This person puts out fires.

construction worker

This person fixes pipes under the road.

People help each other in my town.

crossing guard

STOP

This person helps us cross the street.

librarian

This person helps us find books to read.

10

nurse

This person helps
sick people.

Yes, my town is a good place to live!